SUBJECT INDEX

page

STAINLESS STEEL WARE
   Advantages of Stainless Steel Ware
                                                28
   How to Care for Stainless Steel Ware
                                                1

IMPORTANT: Before using your Stainless Steel Cookware, read page 1 for valuable hints on how to keep your cookware free from scratches, stains and warping.

Au Gratin Vegetables
                                                19
Bananas,
   As garnish
                                                26
   Pan Fried
                                             10, 13
BEEF
   Frizzled Beef
                                                12
   Pot Roast with Vegetables
                                                8
   Roasting Timetable
                                                6
   Standing Rib Roast
                                                7
   Swedish Meat Balls
                                                9
   Swiss Steak
                                                11
Beets, Harvard

Busy Day Supper Dish	20
Care of Stainless Steel Cookware	22
Chicken, Fried	1
Chili Con Carne	14
Christmas Plum Pudding	15
Creamed Vegetables	27
DESSERTS	19
Apricot Whip	
Pineapple Upside Down Cake	26
Plum Pudding	25
Eggplant, Pan-Fried	27
Eggs Benedict	19
Fish, Fried Fillets	23
Food Buying Hints	16
Frosting, Pastel Plum	2
Frozen Meats	24
Frozen Vegetables	6
Gravy, Quick	19
Ham, Diced	22

Busy Day Supper Dish	22
Hollandaise Sauce	23
Jelly, Plum	24
Lamb, Roasting Timetable	6
Meal Planning	3, 4
Meats	5-6
Pineapple Upside Down Cake	25
Plum Jelly	24
Plum Pudding	27
PORK	
Roasting Timetable	6
Stuffed Pork Chops	13
Quick Meal Preparation	4
Roasting Timetable	6
SAUCES	
Custard Sauce	26
Hollandaise Sauce	23
Tartar Sauce	16
Spaghetti, Italian	17
Summer Squash, Pan-Fried	

VEAL
Roasting Timetable — 19

Veal in Mushroom Sauce — 6

VEGETABLES
Frozen Vegetables — 21

General Cooking Hints — 19

Harvard Beets — 18-19

Time-Table — 20

Vegetable Platter — 19

— 20

HOW TO CARE FOR STAINLESS COOKWARE

Stainless Cookware will retain original gleaming beauty through a lifetime of service. Just follow these simple directions:

BEFORE USING NEW UTENSILS—Wash them thoroughly both inside and out in hot suds. Use either soap or detergent. This removes the thin coating of oil which clings to the utensil in the manufacturing process. Rinse in clear hot water and dry thoroughly with a clean towel. Now the utensil is ready for use.

HEAT CONTROL—Medium to Low Heat should be used for all cooking. Start vegetables over medium heat. When the water comes to a boiling, turn to low heat to keep water boiling gently. Brown meat slowly over medium to low heat.

EASY CLEANING—Rinse the utensil with warm water immediately after each use. Food particles which do not yield to rinsing usually may be removed with a rubber food scraper.

FIRST AID—If food has been burned on or allowed to dry on the utensil, fill it with cold water. Bring the water to boiling. Remove the utensil from the heat and allow the water to cool to lukewarm. Wash in hot suds. If a stain remains, scour with fine steel wool. If necessary, polish with stainless steel cleaner.

DO NOT OVERHEAT—Overheating may sometimes cause discoloration on Stainless Steel Cookware. These stains are easily removed with any good stainless steel cleaner.

AVOID SUDDEN TEMPERATURE CHANGES—Sudden temperature changes and overheating should be avoided. DO NOT put cold water in a hot utensil. DO NOT set a hot utensil on a cold surface, such as the sink.

SPEND *Wisely*, SPEND *Less*!

Take Advantage of Bargains

A really big step towards economical food buying is watching newspaper advertisements. Each week the big super-markets and chain stores run all of their weekly specials, and savings will add up fast if you plan as many of your menus as possible around these featured items.

Compare Prices

Compare them at home in your newspaper, when you are deciding the best place to shop and save. And compare the difference in price among fresh, frozen, and canned foods. For example; food dollars will go a lot further (yet meals will not suffer), if you serve frozen vegetables, or fresh vegetables in season, on-the-plate ... and use less-expensive canned vegetables in stews, casseroles, etc.

Read Labels Carefully

Look for the word "enriched" on white bread and flour labels. This means that the "B" vitamins and Iron, lost in the milling process, have been replaced. Also check the "net weight" when comparing similar bargains.

Avoid Waste

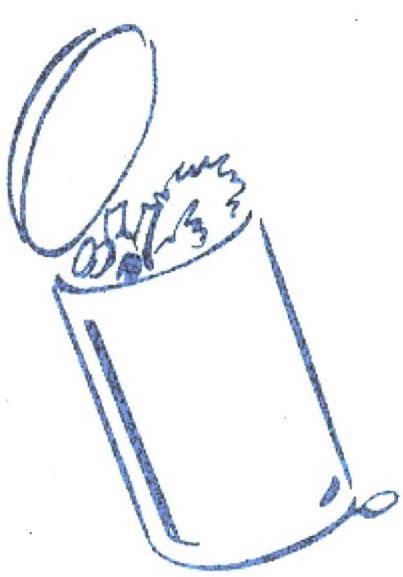

Extra-large sizes of canned fruits, vegetables, juices and staples like baking powder may not ALWAYS be bargains. Often these purchases are only partially used, and eventually go to waste. Unless you can use the entire contents of the extra-large container, buy the smaller size.

Cut Meat Costs

Less tender cuts of meat are just as nutritious as the more expensive ones. Properly cooked they are equally delicious, and you'll be surprised how often you can work them into well-planned menus.

Variety meats, such as heart, kidney, sweetbreads, brain, liver and tongue are high in nutritive value and comparatively low in price.

Butter or Margarine?

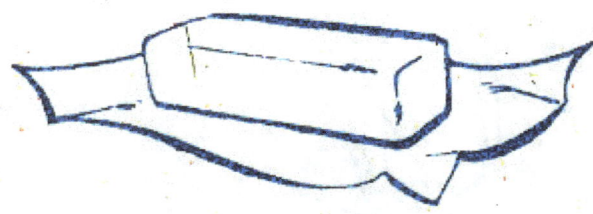

These two table fats are equivalent in food value, and may be used interchangeably in any recipe.

Plan TO PLEASE!

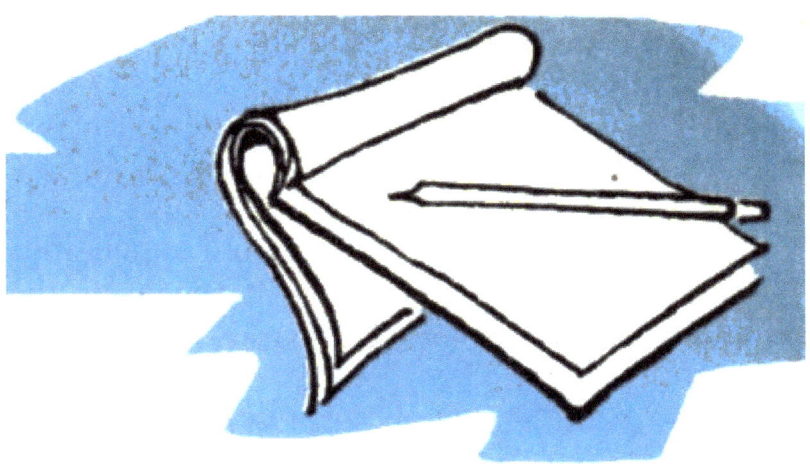

Plan meals when you are a little hungry ... your culinary imagination is better then. Articles in magazines and newspapers help provide inspiration when you need it, for greater menu variety.

When there are small children in the family, it is easier to plan meals around the type of food small-fry can eat. Adults, too, enjoy this simple food, which can be served in attractive and tempting combinations.

Plan the whole day's meals as a unit. This is the only way you can be sure of providing the proper amount of the right kind of food.

These are the foods needed every day for good health:

MILK—3 or 4 cups for children; 2 to 3 cups for adults. Milk used in cooking may be counted in the total.

VEGETABLES and FRUITS—1 serving of green, leafy or yellow vegetable; 1 serving of citrus fruit; 1 serving of potato; 1 other vegetable or fruit, preferably raw. Noodles, spaghetti and macaroni cannot be considered substitutes for potatoes. True, they are high in starch, but important minerals and vitamins found in potatoes are lacking.

MEAT, FISH, POULTRY or CHEESE—1 serving daily.

EGGS—at least 4 a week; 1 daily is better.

Enriched or whole grain **CEREALS** and **BREAD**—2 servings or more.

BUTTER or MARGARINE—2 tablespoons or more.

EYE APPEAL—Colorful combinations are more appetizing. As you plan a menu, try to visualize the food as it will appear on the table. Strive for good contrast of flavor, color, and texture.

OFF THE BEATEN TRACK—Now and then introduce the family to a new food, or an old favorite in new guise. But don't overdo it. One new food at a meal is enough.

DESSERT—Dessert is actually a part of the meal and should always be planned as such. Serve a light dessert when the main course is hearty. Serve rich cake and pie only when the main course is not too filling.

LITTLE EXTRAS—A few sprigs of parsley go a long way to make the meat platter more attractive. A sprinkling of paprika provides a flourish of color for creamed dishes.

A tray of raw relishes ... carrot sticks, celery curls, green pepper rings, radish roses and cucumbers cut lengthwise into fingers ... may pinch-hit for the salad occasionally.

Used with discretion, food coloring is a boon to the cook. Add a few drops of yellow coloring to chicken gravy; a few drops of red coloring to step up the eye appeal of desserts made with canned cherries.

SUPPER IN A *Half-hour*!

Every homemaker needs two or three quick supper dishes "to fall back on" when kitchen time is limited. They can be hearty and attractive, as well as inexpensive.

Following are four such supper menus, easily prepared in about half an hour. Three of them are planned around canned meat, dried beef and corned beef, which should always be kept on hand for emergency meals.

Fruit in season, quick-frozen fruit, or canned fruit, well chilled, always makes a tempting dessert. Strawberry shortcake is an all season quick dessert, with frozen strawberries and individual sponge cakes made especially for this purpose by professional bakers.

Tomato Juice Cocktail
Busy Day Supper Dish (page 22)
Tossed Chef's Salad
Hard Rolls
Butter
Fresh or Frozen Peaches

• • • • • •

Frizzled Beef (page 12)
Buttered Carrots
Head Lettuce Salad
Roquefort Dressing
Pumpernickel Bread
Butter
Orange Sherbet
Cookies

• • • • • • •

Corned Beef Hash with Poached Eggs
Buttered Peas
Tossed Green Salad
French Bread
Butter
Chilled Fruit Cup

• • • • • • •

Hamburger Platter (page 10)
Emergency Gravy (page 22)
Cole Slaw
Toasted English Muffins
Strawberry Shortcake

PREPARING *Meats*

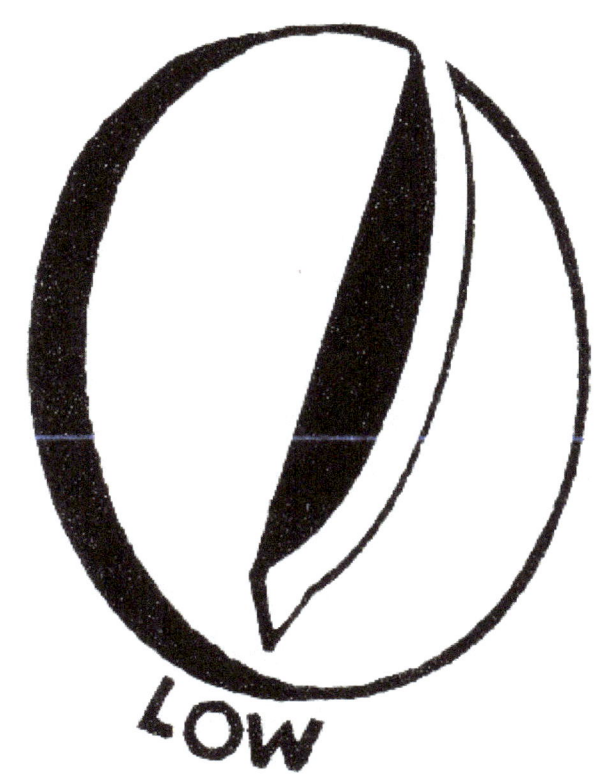

Cooking meat at a low temperature retains juices, reduces the amount of shrinkage and improves the flavor. The theory that searing seals-in juices has been disproved.

Tender cuts of meat are cooked by dry heat: roasting, pan-frying, broiling, pan-broiling.

Less-tender cuts are cooked by moist heat: braising, stewing, soup-making.

ROASTING—Place meat in Dutch oven, fat side up. Season with salt. Roast uncovered, in moderate oven (325 degrees) to desired degree of doneness. Do not add water; do not baste. Roast will be nicely browned by the time cooking is completed. The use of a meat thermometer is recommended. For easier carving, let meat stand in warm place 20 to 30 minutes before serving.

BROILING—Place meat on greased broiler rack. Broil steaks and chops two inches thick three inches away from source of heat. Cuts one inch thick should be placed two inches from heat. Cook until meat is nicely browned on top. Season and turn to brown other side. Season and serve at once.

PAN-BROILING—Preheat chicken fryer or skillet. Brown meat on both sides turning several times, if necessary. Pour off fat as it accumulates. Do not add water; do not cover. Test for doneness by cutting small slit next to bone. Reduce heat to finish cooking.

PAN-FRYING—Melt a small amount of fat in chicken fryer or skillet. Dip meat in flour or egg and crumb coating. Fry slowly until browned on both sides. Reduce heat to finish cooking, if necessary.

BRAISING—Brown meat slowly in hot fat in chicken fryer or saucepan. Meat may be dipped in flour before browning, if desired. Add a small amount of liquid. Cook at simmering temperature until tender.

STEWING—Cut meat into cubes; brown in hot fat in saucepan. Dredging with flour before browning is a matter of choice. Nearly cover meat with water. Cook, covered, at simmering temperature, until tender.

Corned beef, ham, tongue, etc., are cooked in water to cover without preliminary browning.

NO SMOKE—Never heat fat to the point where it smokes. Keep heat low enough at all times to avoid smoking. For best flavor, brown meat slowly over moderate heat.

BEEF—Tender cuts of beef are cooked either rare, medium or well-done, by dry heat: roasting, pan-broiling or broiling. Less-tender cuts must be cooked to the well-done stage by moist heat (braising or stewing) in order to make them tender.

PORK—All pork cuts are tender but must be cooked to the well-done stage. Roasting is suitable for any of the larger cuts. Pork chops and steaks should be cooked by braising for best results.

LAMB—Roasting, pan-broiling, or broiling are suitable methods to use with lamb because all cuts are tender. The fell, the thin papery membrane which covers the lamb carcass, should not be removed before cooking. Lamb may be cooked rare, medium or well-done according to personal preference.

VEAL—All cuts need to be cooked slowly to the well-done stage in order to make veal tender. Veal may be roasted, braised or stewed. When an egg and crumb coating is used, chops and steaks cut ½-inch thick may be pan-fried successfully. (This must be done slowly over medium to low heat.) (see front cover)

TIMETABLE FOR ROASTING

Poultry and all meat except pork is roasted at 325 degrees. Roast pork at 350 degrees. Times given below are approximate, varying with size and shape of roast. A meat thermometer is recommended for accurate determination of degree of doneness.

MEAT	MINUTES PER POUND
Beef	
Rare	18-20
Medium	22-25
Well-done	27-30
Lamb	30-35
Pork	35-40
Smoked pork	20-30
Veal	30
Chicken	25-30

FROZEN MEAT—It is not necessary to thaw meat before cooking. When meat is frozen solid at the beginning of the cooking process, allow up to twice the usual cooking time.

STANDING RIB ROAST

Select a Standing Rib Roast. Place fat side up in Dutch Oven. Do not add water; do not cover; do not baste. Roast in moderate oven, 325°F.

> Rare   18-20 minutes per pound
> Medium   22-25 minutes per pound
> Well-done   27-30 minutes per pound

For sure results use a meat thermometer. Insert it in the thickest part of the roast, being sure that the bulb does not rest on fat or bone. Use the time periods above as a guide. Remove the roast from the oven when the thermometer reading is "rare," "medium," or "well-done," as you prefer.

Tomato-Bacon Garnish

Halve small tomatoes; cross short strips of bacon on top of each half. Broil until bacon is crisp.

MENU

Standing Rib Roast of Beef
Asparagus Hollandaise (p. 23)
Corn on The Cob
Tossed Green Salad
Lemon Chiffon Pie

BEEF POT ROAST and VEGETABLES

1 tablespoon fat
3 to 4-pound chuck roast
salt and pepper
1½ cups water
4 medium onions
8 small carrots
4 medium potatoes
3 tablespoons flour

1. Melt fat in Dutch oven. Brown meat on all sides in hot fat. Season generously with salt and lightly with pepper.

2. Add water; cover and cook over low heat about 2 hours until meat is nearly tender. Add onions; cook 10 minutes. Add carrots and potatoes; cook 30-35 minutes longer, or until all vegetables are tender.

3. Remove meat and vegetables to platter. Measure stock in Dutch oven; add water to make 1½ cups. Bring to a boil.

4. Blend flour with ⅓ cup water; stir into boiling stock. Stir constantly until thickened. Season, if necessary, with salt. This makes generous servings for 4 with enough meat left over for another meal.

SWEDISH MEAT BALLS

1 pound chopped beef
1 cup soft bread crumbs
1 cup rich milk
1 egg
2 medium onions, chopped
2 teaspoons salt
⅛ teaspoon pepper
¼ teaspoon nutmeg

1. Combine ingredients in order listed; mix thoroughly.

2. Melt 1 tablespoon each shortening and butter in skillet.

3. Form meat mixture into small balls about 1-inch in diameter using teaspoon (mixture is too soft to shape with fingers.)

4. Brown meat balls in hot fat, a few at a time; place in bowl until all have been browned. Add a little extra fat to skillet as needed.

5. To drippings in skillet add 1 cup water. Bring to boil. Blend 1 tablespoon flour with 2 tablespoons cold water; stir into gravy. Stir constantly until thickened.

6. Return meat balls to skillet. Cover; simmer gently ½ hour. Makes 8 servings.

PAN-FRIED BANANAS

6 firm bananas[1]
Salt
¼ cup melted butter or margarine

Keep whole or cut crosswise into halves. Fry bananas slowly in butter or margarine until tender ... easily pierced with a fork ... turning the bananas until evenly browned. Sprinkle lightly with salt. Serve hot as a vegetable.

Meal Suggestions: Pan-Fried Bananas, served as a hot vegetable, are excellent flavor partners with fish, meat, poultry or eggs for luncheon or dinner.

Pan-Fried Bananas with Hamburg Patties and Whole Carrots make an appetizing, colorful and nutritious plate combination. To complete the menu, begin with chilled vegetable juice. With the Hamburg platter, serve hot rolls and a tossed green salad.

For dessert, jelly roll slices with ice cream and coffee.

SWISS STEAK

2 pounds top round, cut 1-inch thick
½ cup flour
1 teaspoon salt
⅛ teaspoon pepper
2 tablespoons fat
1 cup canned tomatoes
2 large onions
Cooked broad noodles

1. Cut meat into serving pieces.

2. Combine flour, salt and pepper. Pound flour mixture into meat, using the edge of a heavy saucer or a mallet designed especially for the purpose.

3. Melt fat in chicken fryer over low heat. Brown meat on both sides; add tomatoes, cover; cook slowly about 1 hour.

4. Cut onions crosswise into half-inch slices. Place on top of meat. Continue to cook, covered, about ½ hour longer, or until meat and onions are tender.

5. Serve on hot noodles with one or two slices of onion on top of each portion of meat. Pour pan drippings over all. Makes 6 servings.

FRIZZLED BEEF

4 tablespoons butter or margarine
1 small green pepper, chopped
1 small onion, finely chopped
1 jar (2½ oz.) dried beef
4 tablespoons flour
2 cups milk

1. Melt butter in skillet. Add chopped pepper and onion. Cover; cook slowly about 5 minutes until onion is tender but not brown. (Cover for 4-quart saucepan fits skillet.)

2. Rinse dried beef with hot water; drain; add; cook slowly 2 or 3 minutes longer.

3. Sprinkle flour over all; stir to distribute flour evenly.

4. Stir in milk. Stir constantly until mixture comes to a boil and sauce thickens.

5. Serve over squares of hot corn bread made with corn muffin mix. Makes 4 to 5 servings.

STUFFED PORK CHOPS

6 thick pork chops
2 cups soft bread crumbs
¼ cup melted butter or margarine
½ cup water
¼ teaspoon salt
¼ teaspoon poultry seasoning, sage or thyme
2 tablespoons minced onion
few grains pepper

1. Cut pocket in pork chops from side next to the bone.

2. Combine next 6 ingredients for stuffing. Fill pockets with stuffing. Brown chops in chicken fryer over low heat.

3. Season with salt and pepper. Add water. Cover; cook over low heat 1 hour. Make gravy from pan drippings.

Makes 6 servings.

MENU

Stuffed Pork Chops
Gravy
Pan-fried Bananas (page 10)
Whipped Potatoes
Buttered Green Beans
Raw Vegetable Relishes
Apple Pie

FRIED CHICKEN

1 frying chicken, disjointed
½ cup vegetable fat
2 tablespoons butter or margarine
½ cup flour
1½ teaspoons onion salt
2 tablespoons water

1. Have chicken cut into serving pieces. Wash thoroughly in cold water but do not soak.

2. Melt vegetable fat and butter over low heat in chicken fryer.

3. Combine flour and onion salt in sturdy paper bag. Place three or four pieces of chicken in the bag. Shake the bag to coat the chicken with flour. Put chicken pieces into hot fat. Repeat until all pieces of chicken are floured.

4. Cook over low heat until browned on one side; turn to brown on all sides evenly. Avoid turning more than necessary.

5. Add water. Cover pan. Cook over low heat for 30 minutes. Uncover; cook 15 minutes longer.

Makes 4 servings.

CHILI CON CARNE

3 tablespoons fat
1 large onion, chopped
1 green pepper, chopped
1 pound ground beef
1 No. 2 can (2½ cups) tomatoes
1 can condensed tomato soup
½ teaspoon paprika
⅛ teaspoon cayenne
1 bay leaf
1 tablespoon chili powder
1 clove garlic
1 teaspoon salt

1 No. 2 can (2½ cups) kidney beans
Raw onion rings (optional)

1. Melt fat in 2-quart saucepan. Brown onion, green pepper and meat in hot fat. Add tomatoes, soup, paprika, cayenne, bay leaf and chili powder. Simmer about 1 hour, adding water if mixture gets too thick.

2. Mash garlic and salt together and stir into mixture. Stir in beans. Heat thoroughly. Garnish with onion rings. Makes 6 servings.

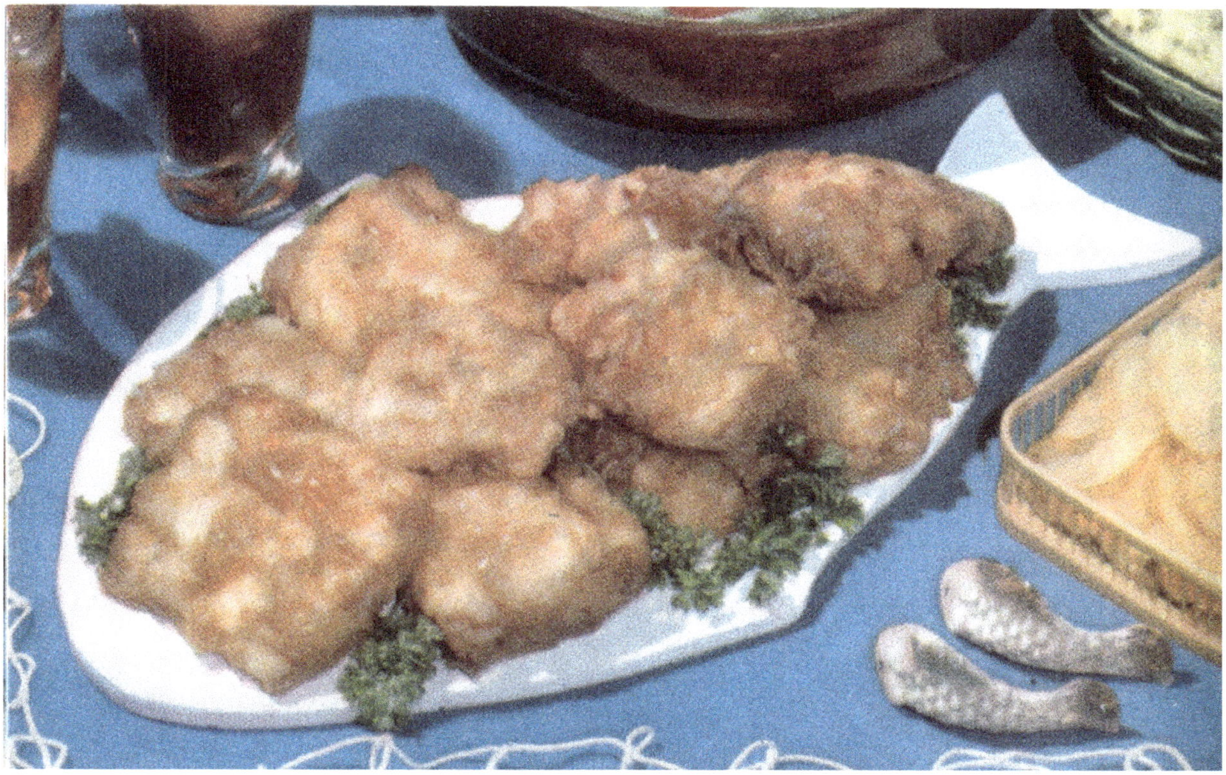

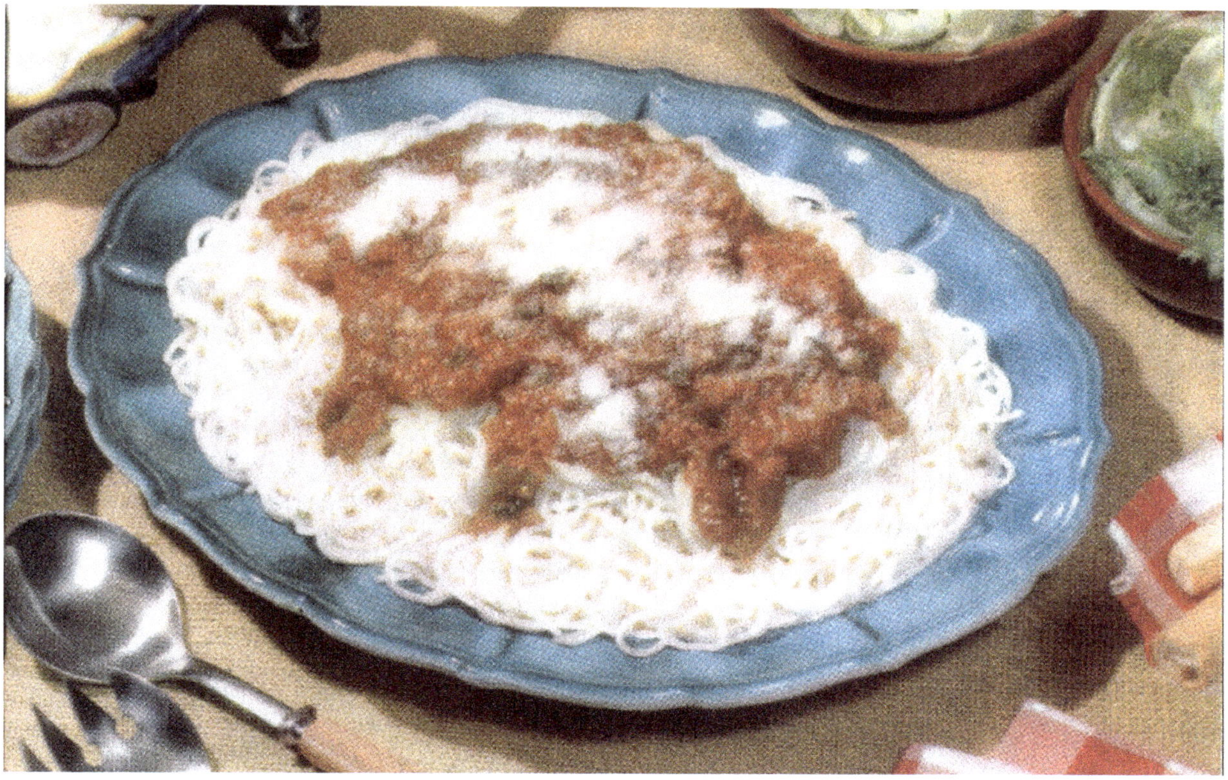

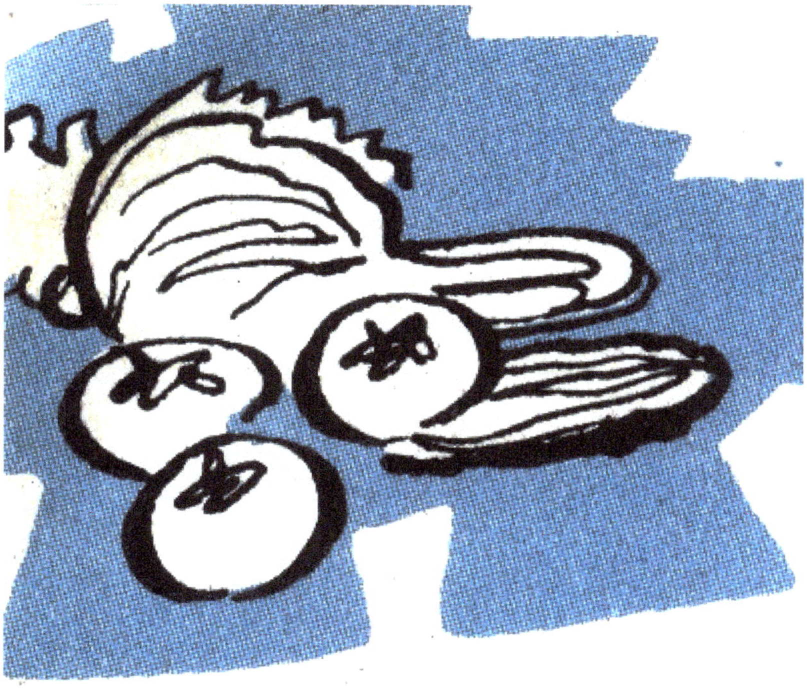

Prepare cauliflower, lima beans, carrots and string beans according to directions on pages 18 and 19. Arrange seasoned vegetables in an attractive pattern on serving platter or chop plate. Top cauliflower with hot mayonnaise or Hollandaise Sauce (page 23).

HARVARD BEETS

   2 tablespoons butter or margarine
   2 tablespoons flour
   ¼ cup boiling water
   1 No. 2 can (2½ cups) sliced beets
   ⅓ cup brown sugar
   ⅛ teaspoon cloves
   ¼ cup vinegar
   ½ teaspoon salt
   few grains pepper

Melt butter or margarine in saucepan. Add flour; blend. Add water and liquid drained from beets; cook until thickened, stirring constantly. Add remaining ingredients except beets, stir until sugar dissolves. Add beets. Heat thoroughly.

VEAL IN MUSHROOM SAUCE

1 pound veal stew meat
2 tablespoons fat
½ teaspoon salt
½ cup water
1 can condensed mushroom soup
1 4-oz. can sliced mushrooms

1. Cut veal into 1½-inch cubes. Melt fat over low heat in 2-quart saucepan. Brown veal slowly, stirring frequently.

2. Add salt and water. Cook, covered, over low heat until tender.

3. Stir in undiluted mushroom soup and drained sliced mushrooms. Heat thoroughly. If necessary, thin gravy with liquid from mushrooms. Serve in Rice Ring. Makes 4 servings.

RICE RING

3 cups hot, cooked rice
4 tablespoons butter or margarine
¼ teaspoon nutmeg
2 tablespoons chopped parsley (optional)

Combine all ingredients. Turn into ring mold. Pack down lightly with spoon. Let stand 2 to 3 minutes. Turn out on serving dish. Or use 2 spoons to shape rice into ring on serving dish.

BUSY DAY SUPPER DISH

1 pkg. frozen asparagus cuts
1 cup cooked diced ham or canned luncheon meat
2 cups well-seasoned medium white sauce

1. Cook asparagus according to directions on package; drain.

2. Stir meat and asparagus into white sauce. Heat thoroughly.

3. Serve on hot split baking powder biscuits.

Makes 4 servings.

Or, serve left-over meat and vegetables in this gravy:

EMERGENCY GRAVY

    1 beef bouillon cube
    1 cup hot water
    2 tablespoons flour
    Kitchen Bouquet
    Salt and pepper

1. Dissolve bouillon cube in hot water; set aside.

2. Melt fat in saucepan or skillet. Stir in flour. Cook over low heat, stirring constantly, until bubbling.

3. Stir in bouillon. Stir constantly until thickened and smooth. Season to taste with Kitchen Bouquet, salt and pepper. Makes 1 cup.

EGGS BENEDICT

Split, toast and butter 6 English muffins. Top each half with thin slice fried ham, one poached egg and Hollandaise Sauce.

HOLLANDAISE SAUCE

⅓ cup butter or margarine
2 egg yolks
⅛ teaspoon salt
few grains pepper
⅓ cup boiling water
1 tablespoon lemon juice

1. Melt butter or margarine in double-boiler. Remove top section of double-boiler.

2. Add egg yolks, one at a time, to melted butter, stirring with a wooden spoon until thoroughly blended.

3. Add salt and pepper. Add boiling water *slowly* while stirring.

4. Set over hot water again. Heat slowly, stirring constantly until mixture is thick and custardlike (about 10 minutes). *Do not let water boil.*

5. Remove from heat; stir in lemon juice. Serve at once.

PLUM JELLY

3 cups prepared juice
4 cups sugar
1 box powdered fruit pectin

TO PREPARE THE JUICE: crush 1 lb. fully ripe plums. (Do not peel or pit). Add ¾ cup water, bring to boil; simmer, covered, 10 minutes. Place in jelly cloth or bag; squeeze out juice. Measure 3 cups into very large saucepan.

TO MAKE THE JELLY: measure sugar; set aside. Place saucepan holding juice over high heat. Add powdered fruit pectin; stir until mixture comes to a hard boil. At once stir in sugar. *Bring to full rolling boil; boil* *hard 1 minute*, stirring constantly. Remove from heat, skim, pour quickly into glasses. Paraffin at once. Makes about 7 six-ounce glasses.

PASTEL PLUM FROSTING: Combine ⅓ cup plum jelly, 1 egg white and dash of salt in top of double-boiler. Beat with rotary egg beater until mixed. Set over boiling water; beat constantly 3 minutes or until frosting "peaks". Cool. Spread on cake.

PINEAPPLE UPSIDE DOWN CAKE

6 tablespoons butter or margarine
⅔ cup brown sugar
1 No. 2 can (2 cups) crisp-cut crushed pineapple
Maraschino cherries
Pecan halves
1 package white cake mix

1. Melt butter or margarine in 9-inch skillet. Sprinkle with brown sugar; top with drained pineapple; decorate with a pattern of Maraschino cherries and pecan halves.

2. Prepare cake mix as directed on package. Pour batter evenly into skillet. Bake in moderate oven, 350°F., 1 hour. Remove from oven. Run spatula around edges of cake. Invert on serving plate. Serve warm with whipped cream or ice cream. Makes 6 to 8 servings.

VARIATIONS

For delightful flavor, try Devil's Food or Spice Cake Mix to make this dessert.

APRICOT WHIP

2 egg whites
⅓ cup sugar
1 tablespoon lemon juice
2 tablespoons fruit juice
few grains salt
½ cup apricot pulp

1. Combine all ingredients except apricot pulp in top of double boiler. Beat with rotary beater to blend.

2. Set over boiling water. Beat until mixture forms peaks.

3. Fold in fruit. Turn into serving dishes. Chill.

4. Garnish with banana slices; serve with Custard Sauce.

CUSTARD SAUCE

    1 cup milk
    2 tablespoons sugar
    ⅛ teaspoon salt
    2 egg yolks (or 1 whole egg)

1. Scald milk in double boiler.

2. Mix salt, egg yolks and sugar in mixing bowl.

3. Stir hot milk into egg mixture. Return to double boiler.

4. Cook, stirring, over hot water, until mixture coats spoon.

5. Pour custard sauce into dish to cool. Stir in ¼ teaspoon vanilla.

CHRISTMAS PLUM PUDDING

1 cup seedless raisins
1½ cups mixed diced candied fruits and peels
½ cup chopped walnuts
1 cup sifted enriched flour
2 eggs, beaten
¾ cup molasses
¾ cup buttermilk
½ cup finely chopped suet
¼ cup grapejuice
1 cup fine dry bread crumbs
¾ teaspoon baking soda
¼ teaspoon allspice

¼ teaspoon cloves
¼ teaspoon cinnamon
¼ teaspoon nutmeg
¾ teaspoon salt

Combine raisins, fruits and peels, walnuts and ½ cup of the flour.

Combine eggs, molasses, buttermilk, suet and grapejuice. Combine remaining flour, crumbs, baking soda, spices and salt; add to egg mixture. Add floured fruit; mix well. Pour into well-greased 1½ quart melon mold; cover; set on rack in deep kettle; add boiling water to about one inch below cover of mold. Cover. Steam 1½ to 2 hours. Makes 10 to 12 servings.

Shape hard sauce into balls; roll in coconut; chill.

HERE'S HOW YOUR STAINLESS STEELWARE SAVES FOOD VALUES

STAINLESS STEEL, the most modern development in metallurgical science, is wonderful for any type of cooking. America's largest canneries, food processors and the better restaurants cook and process food in stainless steel utensils. Stainless steel not only preserves natural food flavors ... it is also easiest to keep sanitary and is immune to wear.

USE YOUR STAINLESS STEELWARE FOR

HEALTHFUL WATER-LESS COOKING
(cooking with minimum amount of water)

The Water-Less way of cooking is highly recommended by leading health and home economics authorities.

Heavy-weight Stainless Steel construction and seal-tight covers assure perfect Water-Less cooking results. Meats and vegetables cooked the Water-Less way (cooking with minimum amount of water) retain their precious mineral elements and vitamins ... and this modern method also preserves the natural flavors and color of the food.

WAYS TO USE LEFT-OVERS

If it's good food, don't throw it away. Little left-overs, or big ones, fit into many dishes; adding extra food value or a fresh new touch to favorite main dishes. Listed below are some left-over uses recommended by the Bureau of Human Nutrition and Home Economics, U. S. Department of Agriculture.

EGG YOLKS, in

Cakes
Cornstarch pudding
Custard or sauce
Pie filling
Salad dressing
Scrambled eggs

EGG WHITES, in

Custard
Fruit whip
Meringue
Souffles

HARD COOKED EGG OR YOLK, in

Casserole dishes
Garnish
Salads
Sandwiches

SOUR MILK, in

Cakes, cookies
Quick breads

SOUR CREAM, in

Cakes, cookies
Dessert sauce
Meat stews
Pie filling
Salad dressing
Sauce for vegetables

COOKED POTATOES, in

Croquettes
Fried or creamed potatoes
Meat-pie crust
Potatoes in cheese sauce
Stew or chowder

COOKED CARROTS, LIMA BEANS, CORN, SNAP BEANS, PEAS, in

Meat and vegetable pie

Soup
Stew
Stuffed peppers
Stuffed tomatoes
Vegetables in cheese sauce

COOKED LEAFY VEGETABLES, CHOPPED, in

Creamed vegetables
Soup
Meat loaf
Meat patties
Omelet
Souffle

COOKED OR CANNED FRUITS, in

Fruit cup
Fruit sauces
Jellied fruit
Quick breads
Shortcake
Upside-down cake
Yeast breads

COOKED MEATS, POULTRY, FISH, in

Casserole dishes
Hash
Meat patties
Meat pies
Salads
Sandwiches
Stuffed vegetables

COOKED WHEAT, OAT OR CORN CEREALS, in

Fried cereal

Meat loaf or patties
Sweet puddings

COOKED SPAGHETTI, RICE, NOODLES, in

Casseroles
Meat or cheese loaf
Timbales

BREAD

Slices, for
    French toast
Dry crumbs, in
    Brown betty
    Croquettes
    Fried chops
Soft crumbs, in
    Meat loaf
    Stuffings

CAKE OR COOKIES, in

Brown betty
Ice-box cake
Toasted, with sweet topping, for dessert